# Baby Knits
## Toys

igloobooks

Published in 2015
by Igloo Books Ltd
Cottage Farm
Sywell
NN6 0BJ
www.igloobooks.com

Cover images © Thinkstock / Getty Images

LEO002 1015
2 4 6 8 10 9 7 5 3
ISBN 978-1-78440-280-8

Printed and manufactured in China

# Baby Knits

## Toys

# Contents

# Introduction

Knitting for babies is a particular favourite with knitters of all levels, not just because of the small and sweet designs, but because of the inherently personal quality that comes with a lovingly woven hand-knitted item. Baby knits are the perfect way to commemorate the arrival of a precious newborn, whether you're knitting for your own baby or for a family member or friend. Imagine receiving such an affectionately crafted gift for your child, to be worn or played with and cherished for years to come. Baby knits are a joy to receive and a joy to knit, and are highly rewarding little projects.

This book presents an adorable range of knitted toys for babies, ideally sized for little hands to hold. This charming collection will inspire knitters of all abilities to create something small but beautiful.

Each pattern is illustrated with adorable photographs, alongside clear instructions and charts and diagrams where necessary. The helpful introduction provides an illustrated guide to basic stitches and knitting skills for new knitters, together with an overview of the essentials in knitting tools and terminology.

This guide contains everything you will need to create gorgeous, soft and truly special baby knits.

# Learn to knit:
# Knitting Essentials

Learning the lingo, understanding needle sizes and being able to change colours are essentials that every keen knitter should know.

Knitting is an enjoyable and rewarding hobby, but sometimes it can be daunting. It may look like a world of meaningless letters and confusing numbers but by learning the lingo and becoming familiar with the tools and techniques, it will all make sense. Knitting abbreviations are one of the trickiest elements of the knitting world, but 'k2tog' does actually mean something. The list opposite will decipher the code and it will soon be second nature.

Needles come in a wide variety of sizes. They are your most vital tool so it is important that you know your 6s from your 6mm. Thin needles are required for small and fine projects whereas larger needles are used for chunkier tasks.

The chart opposite will help you choose the right needle for your project. We will also guide you through the basics of changing colour for when you are ready to move on.

| Needle Conversion Chart | | |
| --- | --- | --- |
| mm | UK | US |
| 2.0 mm | 14 | 0 |
| 2.25 mm | 13 | 1 |
| 2.5 mm | 12 | |
| 2.75 mm | 12 | 2 |
| 3.0 mm | 11 | 3 |
| 3.25 mm | 10 | 3 |
| 3.5 mm | 9 | 4 |
| 3.75 mm | 9 | 5 |
| 4.0 mm | 8 | 6 |
| 4.5 mm | 7 | 7 |
| 5.0 mm | 6 | 8 |
| 5.5 mm | 5 | 9 |
| 6.0 mm | 4 | 10 |
| 6.5 mm | 3 | 10½ |
| 7.0 mm | 2 | |
| 7.5 mm | 1 | |
| 8.0 mm | 0 | 11 |
| 9.0 mm | 00 | 13 |
| 10 mm | 000 | 15 |

## Changing Colour

Changing colour to create stripes is most easily done at the end of a row. First, knit all the rows that you need to, with your first colour.

When you are ready to change colour, drop the old colour. Pick up the new colour by threading the beginning of the new colour through the back of the last stitch and pulling the old colour tightly, trapping the new colour.

Hold both the start of the new colour and the end of the old colour together and resume knitting as normal, using the new colour. After every row, pull the end of the new colour to keep it tight, but ensure that the tension is kept even. Cut the old colour, leaving a 15cm/6in tail. Use a tapestry needle to weave the loose ends in.

## Abbreviations

| | | | | | |
|---|---|---|---|---|---|
| **alt** | alternate | **m1** | make one* | **sl1** | slip 1 st |
| **approx.** | approximately | **m1l** | make one left | **skpo** | sl1, k1, pass sl st over |
| **beg** | beginning | **m1r** | make one right | **sm** | slip marker |
| **CC** | contrast colour | **m1p** | make one purl | **ssk** | slip first st, slip second st, then knit both together off right-hand needle |
| **cont** | continue | **MC** | main colour | | |
| **dec** | decrease(ing) | **N1/N2** | needle 1/needle 2 | | |
| **DPN** | double-pointed needle | **p** | purl | **st(s)** | stitch(es) |
| **foll** | following | **p2tog** | purl 2 together | **st st** | stocking stitch |
| **folls** | follows | **patt** | pattern | **tbl** | through back loop |
| **g st** | garter stitch | **pm** | place marker | **tog** | together |
| **inc** | increase(ing) | **psso** | pass slipped st over | **w&t** | wrap and turn |
| **k** | knit | **pwise** | purlwise | **wyif** | with yarn in front |
| **k2tog** | knit 2 together | **rem** | remain(ing) | **WS** | wrong side |
| **kfb** | knit into front and back of stitch | **rep** | repeat | **yf** | yarn forward |
| **KTS** | knit the steek st | **rnd** | round | **yo** | yarn over |
| **kwise** | knitwise | **RH** | right hand | **yon** | yarn over needle |
| **LH** | left hand | **RS** | right side | **yrn** | yarn round needle |

*make one by lifting the bar between sts, placing it onto the LH needle and knitting into the back of the lifted bar

# Learn to knit:
# The Basic Stitches

The following pages contain the basic stitches that you will need to begin knitting. Each how-to section covers a different stitch, with comprehensive step-by-step explanation and accompanying images.

## Long-tail cast on

This uses a single needle and produces an elastic knitted edge like a row of garter stitch.

### Step 1

Leaving an end about three times the length of the required cast-on, put a slipknot on the needle. Holding the yarn end in the left hand, take the left thumb under the yarn and upwards. Insert the needle in the loop just made on the thumb.

### Step 2

Use the ball end of the yarn to make a knit stitch, slipping the loop off the thumb. Pull the yarn end to close the stitch up to the needle. Continue making stitches in this way.

## Chain cast off

A simple knit stitch cast off is used in most of these projects. Knit two stitches. * With the left needle, lift the first stitch over the second. Knit the next stitch. Repeat from * until one stitch remains. Break the yarn, take the end through this stitch and tighten.

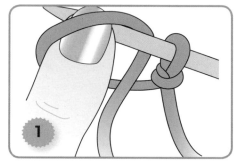

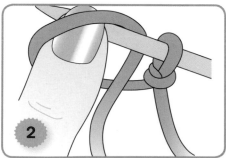

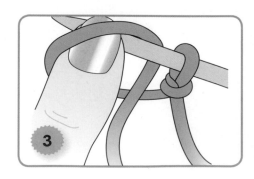

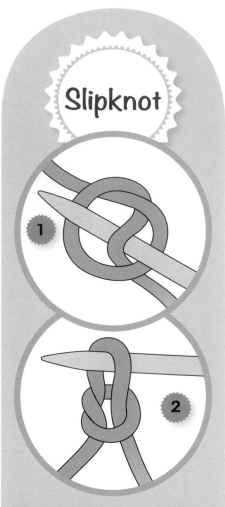

## Slipknot

### Step 1

A slipknot is the first stage of any cast on. Loop the yarn around two fingers of the left hand, the ball end on top. Dip the needle into the loop, catch the ball end of the yarn and pull it through the loop.

### Step 2

Pull the ends of the yarn to tighten the knot. Tighten the ball end to bring the knot up to the needle.

### Ends

The end of yarn left after casting on should be a reasonable length of approx 10–30cm/4–12in so that it can be used for sewing up. The same applies to the end left after casting off.

# Knit Stitch (K)

Choose to hold the yarn and needles in whichever way you feel most comfortable. To create tension in the yarn – that is, to keep it moving evenly – you will need to twist it through some fingers of the hand holding the yarn, and maybe even take it around your little finger. Continuous rows of knit stitch produce garter stitch. It does take some practice to get the stitches even so don't be discouraged, keep on practising.

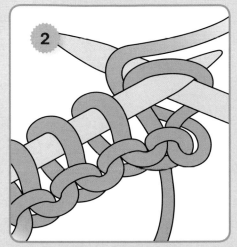

**Step 1**

Insert the right needle into the first stitch on the left needle. Make sure it goes from left to right into the front of the stitch.

**Step 2**

Taking the yarn behind, bring it up and around the right needle.

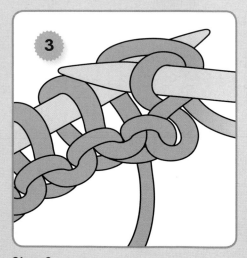

**Step 3**

Using the tip of the right needle, draw a loop of yarn through the stitch.

**Step 4**

Slip the stitch off the left needle. There is now a new stitch on the right needle.

# Purl Stitch (P)

**Step 1**

Insert the right needle into the first stitch on the left needle. Make sure it goes into the stitch from right to left.

**Step 2**

Lower the tip of the right needle, taking it away from you to draw a loop of yarn through the stitch.

**Step 3**

Taking the yarn to the front, loop it around the right needle.

**Step 4**

Slip the stitch off the left needle. There is now a new stitch on the right needle.

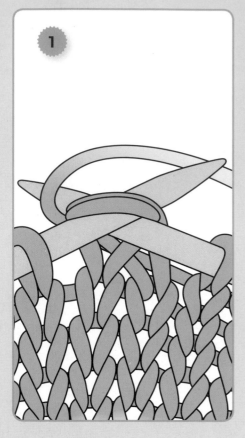

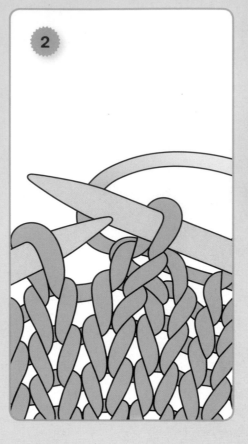

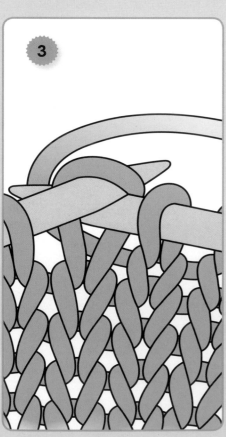

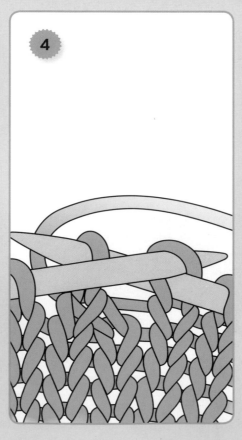

# Decreases

Decreases have two basic functions. They can be used to reduce the number of stitches in a row, as in armholes and necklines, and combined with increases, they can create stitch patterns.

## Right slanting single decreases (k2tog)

Knitting two stitches together makes a smooth shaping, with the second stitch lying on top of the first.

### Step 1

Insert the right needle through the front of the first two stitches on the left needle, then take the yarn around the needle.

### Step 2

Draw the loop through and drop the two stitches off the left needle.

## Left slanting double decreases (sk2po)

For a double decrease that slants to the left, worked on a right-side row, you'll need to take the first stitch over a single decrease. For a similar-looking decrease worked on a wrong-side row, purl three together through the back of the loops (p3tog tbl).

### Step 1

Insert the right needle knitwise through the front of the first stitch on the left needle, and slip it onto the right needle.

### Step 2

Knit the next two stitches together, then lift the first stitch over as shown. To make a right-slanting double decrease, simply knit three stitches together (k3tog).

# Yarn Over (yo)

It's essential to take the yarn over the needle so that the strand lies in the same direction as the other stitches. Working into this strand on the next row makes a hole, but if the strand is twisted, the hole will close up.

When the stitch before a yarn over is purl, the yarn will already be at the front, ready to go over the needle.

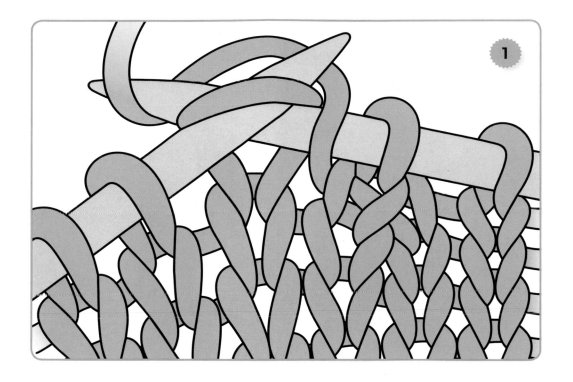

### Step 1

To make a yarn over between knit stitches, bring the yarn to the front as if to purl, then take it over the needle to knit the next stitch.

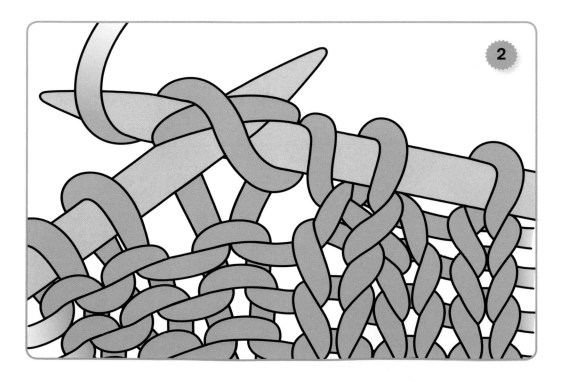

### Step 2

To make a yarn over between a knit and a purl, bring the yarn to the front as if to purl, take it over the needle and bring it to the front again, ready to purl.

# Increases

Here are two of the most basic methods of increasing a single stitch – bar increase and lifted strand increase.

## Bar increase on a knit row (kfb)

Knitting into the front and the back of a stitch is the most common increase. It's a neat, firm increase, which makes a little bar on the right side of the work at the base of the new stitch. This makes it easy to count rows between shapings and doesn't leave a hole.

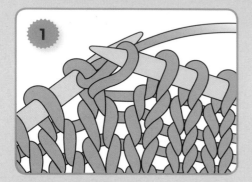

### Step 1

Knit into the front of the stitch and pull the loop through, but leave the stitch on the left needle.

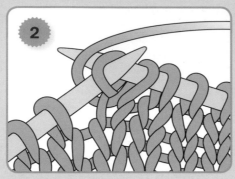

### Step 2

Knit into the back of the stitch on the left needle.

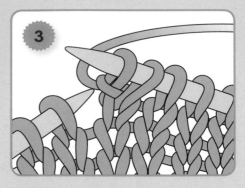

### Step 3

Slip the stitch off the left needle, making two stitches on the right needle. Note that the bar of the new stitch lies on the left.

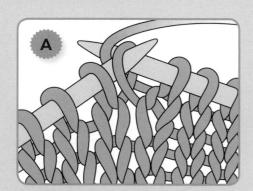

### Lifted strand increase to the left (ml or mlL)

Making a stitch from the strand between stitches is a very neat way to increase.

### Picture A

From the front, insert the left needle under the strand between stitches. Make sure the strand lies on the needle in the same direction as the other stitches, then knit into the back of it.

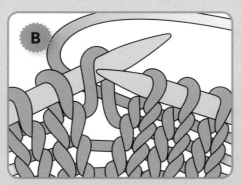

### Lifted strand increase to the right (mlR)

This right-slanting increase balances exactly the lifted strand increase to the left.

### Picture B

From the back, insert the left needle under the strand between the stitches. It will not lie in the same direction as the other stitches, so knit into the front of it.

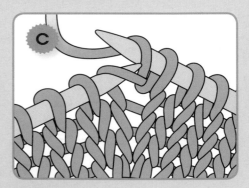

### Double increase

This is one of the simplest ways to make three stitches out of one.

### Picture C

Knit one stitch without slipping it off, take the yarn over the right needle from front to back then knit the same stitch again. A small but decorative hole is left in the fabric.

# Twists

Twisting stitches is working two or three stitches out of sequence, but without using a cable needle. This is an easy way to create patterns where lines of stitches travel over the surface of the knitting.

## Left twist (t2L)

This twist is worked on a right-side row. As the stitches change place, the first stitch lies on top and slants to the left, while the stitch behind is worked through the back of the loop.

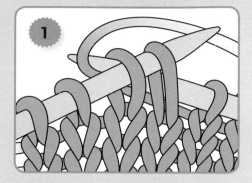 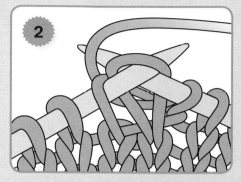 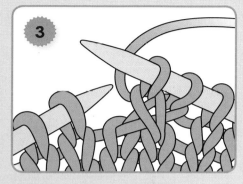

**Step 1**

Knit into the back of the second stitch.

**Step 2**

Knit into the front of the first stitch.

**Step 3**

Slip both stitches off the left needle together.

## Right twist (t2R)

In this right-sided row twist, the second stitch lies on top and slants to the right, while the stitch behind is worked through the back of the loop.

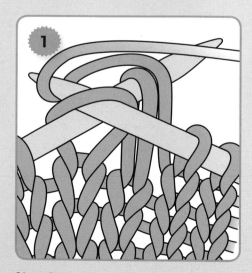 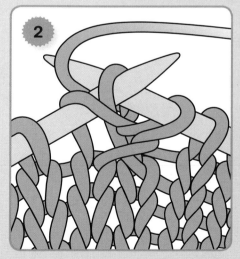 

**Step 1**

Knit into the front of the second stitch.

**Step 2**

Knit into the back of first stitch.

**Step 3**

Slip both stitches off the left needle together.

# Learn to knit:
# Fair Isle

Fair Isle or stranded knitting is a really popular technique and it's easy when you know how.

Traditional Fair Isle may use many colours in the design. However, only two colours are typically used in a row, which makes it less complex to work than it seems. Patterns are worked in stocking stitch from charts, using colours or symbols to indicate each different colour. Charts are read from the bottom, starting at the right-hand side. Each square represents a stitch, each row of squares a row of knitting.

In flat knitting, right side rows are normally worked from right to left, wrong side rows from left to right. Odd-numbered rows will usually be knit, even rows purl. In circular knitting, all rows are read from right to left and, as a rule with Fair Isle, all rows will be knit as the right side of the work is always facing you.

## Yarn

For good pattern definition, a fine Shetland wool is traditionally used, being warm, light and durable. Other wool will work well and Fair Isle patterns can be found on a wide range of projects from fine socks through to heavier sweaters and jackets.

Try swatching non-wool yarns for handle and appearance. Some yarns, especially cottons, can be slippery, which can make maintaining even tension more difficult.

## Colour changing

When changing colours the yarn not in use (the 'float' or 'float yarn') is carried across the wrong side of the work by stranding or weaving in to avoid constantly breaking off and rejoining the yarn.

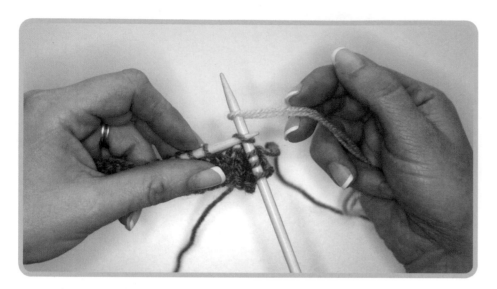

**Knit row**

1. To work the chart shown, starting at the bottom right and working from right to left, knit in colour A (dark blue) until the first colour change. Make the next stitch by joining in colour B (light blue) as normal. Leave a tail of B for darning in later and don't cut off A.

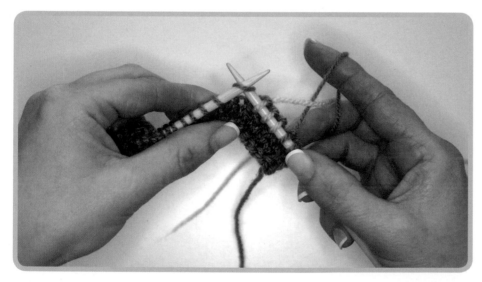

2.   Knit in B to the next colour change. Lift yarn A from beneath, under B, and knit with A until the next colour change. Repeat for each colour change, lifting the new yarn from under the working yarn.

Repeat this process, changing yarn according to the chart until the end of the row. At the end of the row check that when the fabric is slightly stretched, the floats are not pulling the fabric in.

## Stranding

This method works well where colour changes are frequent (no more than four or five stitches apart). It gives a less dense, lighter fabric and uses less yarn than weaving in.

## Weaving in

Weaving in avoids loose floats across the back of the work and the two colours in the row are neatly entwined or woven together at each stitch.

Both techniques have their place. Stranding is ideal for areas with frequent colour changes within the row and where a lighter, less dense fabric is required.

For firmer fabrics, where the floats would be too long or where even short floats would be likely to snag, weaving in may be preferable. With socks or gloves, the floats may catch on rings or between toes. This can be annoying and may spoil your knitting so weaving in may be the better method here for changing colours within the row.

### Purl row

1. Work the next row of the chart from right to left in purl. As with the knit row, lift the new colour from beneath the working yarn at each colour change so the old yarn lies in front of the new yarn as it faces you.

### Weaving in: Knit Row, using B

1. To work a stitch in yarn B (light blue), A (dark blue) is woven in. Insert RH needle to begin a k st as normal. Take A over the top of B and wrap round RH needle as if to knit. Take B around RH needle as if to k. A sits behind B on RH needle.

2. Before completing the k st, bring A back around the RH needle. Note how A now lies over B. Leaving A over B, k the next st as normal in B.

## Semi-stranding or catching in

Sometimes there's a long run of stitches in a single colour. In this case, it's possible to catch in the second colour every three or four stitches using the weaving-in method (left). This differs from the full weaving-in technique because the yarn is only woven in every few stitches rather than every single stitch. This technique may combine better with stranding as it's less dense and better matches the teel and density of a stranded fabric.

The best way to decide which method to use is by swatching. Test each section of the pattern, bearing in mind the type of garment or accessory you're making. Where will the pattern be? Will it get lots of wear? Is it likely to be in an area prone to snagging?

### Can the techniques be combined?

Yes – in fact, with some patterns it may be unavoidable, but you need to swatch carefully. With properly worked swatches, there shouldn't be any difference in tension, but be aware of the feel of the fabric. Be sure to include some rows of single-colour knitting in your swatches if they feature in the pattern as these may also feel slightly different to the coloured sections.

# Learn to knit:
# Double Knitting

Many of us love colourwork but are frustrated by the messy wrong side. This clever technique creates a completely reversible fabric.

Double knitting is a fascinating technique that can be used in a variety of ways. This section looks at using double knitting to create reversible, double-faced fabric where both sides of the fabric are permanently interlocked and joined together.

This kind of double knitting can be worked flat or in the round and colourwork looks stunning. With double knitting, a red star on a white background on one side magically transforms into a white star on a red background when viewed from the other side, and no one will know how you did it!

## How double knitting works

While there's no problem simply following the instructions and accepting that the pattern does what it says on the tin, you may find it helpful when following charts to understand how the technique works. A knit stitch is smooth on the side facing you and has a bump on the reverse. Purl stitches, in contrast, show a bump on the front as it faces you but are smooth on the side facing away from you.

The nature of this knitting technique means that the bumps are trapped between the smooth knit stitches and therefore can't be seen. This leaves only the smooth (right) sides visible on both outer faces of the fabric.

## Terminology

As both sides of the work are effectively the right side, you may find it easier to think of the two sides as A and B. Each yarn will be both main (background) and contrasting (foreground) yarn, so if yarn X is the main colour (MC) on side A, it will be the contrasting colour (CC) on side B.

Yarn Y will then be the CC on side A but the MC on side B. The colours may also be referred to in patterns as MC1 and MC2.

## Casting on

Double knitting patterns normally specify a cast on. If not, you can use any cast on, working with both yarns at the same time. Note that you will cast on twice as many stitches as there are squares in your chart as each square represents two stitches.

Before you begin knitting, make sure that the stitches are in pairs in the same order – for example, all the pairs should be XY. Using both colours will create a two-colour cast-on edge. For a single colour edge, a provisional cast on, such as tubular cast on, can be used.

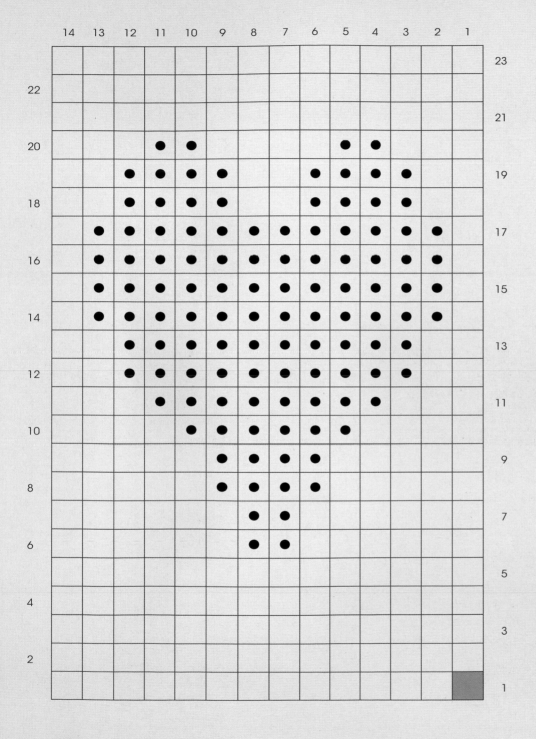

## Reading double knitting charts

Double knitting patterns are usually charted. Unlike in regular knitting, in double knitting each square on the chart represents two stitches.

Depending on the colour of the square, this will determine which colour yarn is knitted and which yarn is purled.

As the two fabrics form a reversible pattern, a stitch knitted on side A in yarn X will give a visible stitch in X on side A. If a stitch is purled using yarn X on side A, this stitch will not be seen on side A but will be visible on side B.

As with other charts, charts for flat knitting read right to left then left to right. For knitting in the round, all rows read right to left.

Start knitting here

Odd rows (side A knit in X (MC1), purl in Y (MC2)
Even rows (side B knit in Y (MC2), purl in X (MC1)

Odd rows (side A knit in Y (MC1), purl in X (MC2)
Even rows (side B knit in X (MC1), purl in Y (MC2)

## Flat and circular knitting

### Step 1

Below the contrasting yarn you will see a series of bumps made in the main yarn (X).

These bumps are picked up in this row, increasing the stitches and forming the stitches for one face of the fabric (side A). The existing stitches form the other face (B).

### Need to know

#### Tubular cast on

Using a piece of smooth contrasting waste yarn, cast on half the total number of stitches needed, plus one extra stitch (You can use the backwards loop method as this is easier to unpick later.)

For our sample chart (see page 21), cast on 15 stitches (total stitches = 28, halved = 14, plus 1 = 15).

#### Set up rows

**Knitting in the round**

Join work into circle, checking that there are no twisted stitches.

Change to yarn X.

**Set Up Row 1:** P2, p2tog, p to end

**Set Up Row 2:** Purl.

Change to yarn Y.

**Set Up Row 3:** Purl.

**Set Up Row 4:** Purl. Purl side should be facing you.

#### Flat knitting

Change to yarn X.

**Set Up Row 1:** P2, p2tog, p to end.

**Set Up Row 2:** Knit.

Change to yarn Y.

**Set Up Row 3:** Purl.

**Set Up Row 4:** Knit. Purl side should be facing you.

## Step 2

**Chart Row 1 (Side A):** *With RH needle, lift bump of main yarn (X) below contrasting yarn, place on LH needle and ktbl. Bring both yarns X (MC1) and Y (MC2) to front of work and p next stitch using just yarn Y. Repeat from * to last stitch.

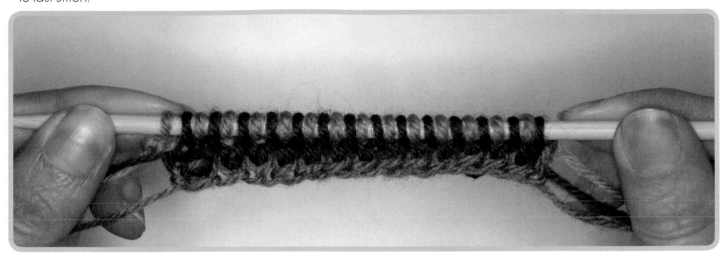

## Step 3

Check you have the correct number of stitches before proceeding. The final stitch should be a purl to maintain the pairing of stitches. For flat knitting, turn to work side B (chart row 2). For knitting in the round, place a marker and continue knitting round 2 (chart row 2) without turning the work. Note that you will have twice the number of stitches as squares shown in the chart (28 sts, 14 squares on the chart). This is because each square represents two stitches. The waste yarn can be carefully removed after several rows have been worked.

## Flat knitting

## Step 4

Hold both yarns to the back of the work, but knit the next stitch in just yarn Y.

## Step 5

Bring both yarns to front of work. Keeping both yarns at the front, but using yarn X (MC1) only, purl next stitch. The first chart square is now completed.

## Finishing a row (flat knitting only)

When working flat/straight (as opposed to knitting in the round), you will need to make a neat finish to the edges. For a tidy edge with a neat, solid line of each colour running up the sides, try the following technique:

### Step 6

Repeat steps 4 and 5 to last square on chart. Two stitches on LH needle. Keeping both yarns at back of work, slip next stitch purlwise (as if to purl).

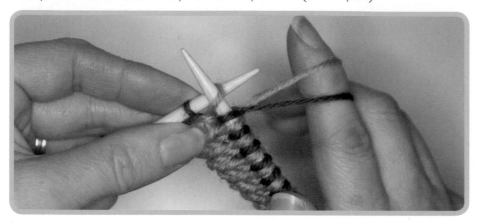

### Step 7

Bring yarn that is the same colour as the final stitch (X in this case), to the front of work. (One yarn either side of work). Keeping just this one yarn to the front, slip final stitch purlwise.

The side facing you (B) will have a row of smooth stitches in colour Y (MC2), the side facing away from you (A) will have a row of smooth stitches in colour X (MC1). Purl stitches worked in X (MC1) produce a barely visible bump on side B facing you but are visible and smooth when viewed on side A.

### Step 8

Turn the work. One yarn (Y in this case) is in front, facing you and one is at the back, away from you (X). Knit first stitch in the same colour as the final stitch of the last row (X in this case).

## Hints & tips

You may be working an X colour stitch over a Y colour stitch, even though you are working a block of a single colour (see steps 11 and 12). Don't worry – if you are following the pattern it will turn out correctly! Focus on which is the MC and which is the CC for the side you are on and not the colour of the next stitch on the LH needle.

Remember that, irrespective of the colours being used, stitch pairings are always knit, purl. You shouldn't have any knit (or purl) stitches together.

The chart should have a clearly explained key but it may help to write out the key with your choice of colours written on to keep you on track.

## Step 9

Bring X (MC1) to the front. Both yarns are now together at the front of the work. Purl next stitch with just yarn Y (MC2).

## Step 10

Take both yarns to back and continue to work rest of row, knitting in X (MC1), purling in Y (MC2). By working in this way at the end of each row, after several rows you will see a neat row of chain stitches up each side of the work.

## Knitting in the round

Repeat steps 4 and 5 following chart (see page 15), but, because you are always working with side A facing you, work knit stitches in X (MC1) and purls in Y (MC2), still with two stitches for each square on chart.
Mark end of round with a stitch marker.

The side facing you (A) will have a row of smooth stitches in colour X (MC1), the side facing away from you (B) will have a row of smooth stitches in colour Y (MC2). Purl stitches worked in Y (MC2) produce a barely visible bump on side A facing you but are visible and smooth when viewed on side B.

Repeat steps 4 and 5 following chart (see page 15)

### Hints & tips

Some patterns will specify a cast on, in which case it is advisable to use the specified method. If no method is specified, the tubular cast on worked in a single colour will give a neat edge to match the slipped stitch side edges

Practise working with both yarns over your finger as this helps to keep the tension even and also makes it easier to ensure that you always bring both yarns back and forwards together

If you spot a stray bar across a stitch this means you have left a yarn behind when moving front to back or vice versa and the work will need to be taken back to the appropriate point

## Step 11

The next pair of stitches need to produce a visible stitch in CC (Y on this row). To produce a visible stitch we need to knit it, so if we want a visible stitch in Y we have to knit the next stitch in Y.

## Step 12

We don't want to see the next stitch on this side of the work so it is purled using X.

## Step 13

Repeat this process for each CC square on the chart. When a square is shown in MC, work these stitches by knitting in X and purling in Y. Note that we are still working knit, purl, but we will have two same-colour stitches next to one another at each colour change.

### Need to know

## Working patterns and motifs

When you reach the first pattern row for the motif, it helps if you think in terms of main colour (MC) and contrast colour (CC). Unlike other colourwork, there are no solid runs of a single colour since every chart square is worked twice and every square will always be worked once in each colour. What changes is not the order of knit and purl (this always stays the same) but which colour of the pair you use to knit with and which colour you purl with.

Looking at Row 6 in our chart, whether you are working flat or in the round, the motif begins with side A facing you. The knit stitches on this side (A) were worked in yarn X, so X is our MC for this face of the work. Yarn Y is therefore the CC. Work as above, working the knit stitches in X and purling the paired stitches in Y until you reach the colour change.

## Casting off

## Step 14

For a neat cast off, grafting (kitchener stitch) is a great choice. For this, you will need two double-pointed needles (DPNs) in the same size as your main knitting. Work to within one row of the end of the pattern. Holding 2 DPNs parallel in your RH, slip knit stitches onto front needle and purl stitches onto back needle. To avoid a stepped finish, work one row of purl on just the stitches on the back needle. Don't turn the work but slide the knitting back to the RH end of the DPNs. Graft the two edges together as normal. Whereas on side B the heart is in yarn X with the background in Y, when viewed from side A, the heart is in yarn Y with the background in X.

### Need to know

### Flat knitting

At the end of the row, follow the steps for finishing a row as above, then work side B. As side B has Y as the MC, X is the CC, so work all MC squares with the knit stitch in Y and the purl stitch in X. Work CC squares with X as the knit stitch and Y as the purl stitch.

**Note:** Remember that in flat knitting, rows on a chart are worked right to left, then left to right.

### Knitting in the round

When knitting projects in the round, there will be no edge stitches so no need to perform any slipped stitch manoeuvres at the end of the round and you can ignore the section for finishing a row (above).

Charts for knitting in the round are always worked from right to left so you will always have side A facing you. This makes things easier as the MC and CC will remain the same throughout.

# Learn to knit:
# Cable Knitting

Knitting groups of stitches out of sequence creates exciting stitch patterns. Cables can be worked with two or more stitches and crossed to the front or the back.

For rich texture and dramatic shape it is impossible to ignore cables. In their simplest terms, cables are essentially combinations of knit and purl stitches worked out of sequence.

Cables can be worked in an endless variety of sizes and combinations. Stitches are transferred to a short needle (a cable needle) and these stitches are then held either at the front or the back of the knitting.

A number of stitches are then knitted from the main needle. To complete the sequence, the stitches from the cable needle are then knitted.

This has the effect of creating a crossed fabric. Where stitches are held at the back the cross will be to the right. Stitches held at the front will create a cross moving to the left.

## What are cables?

Cables are usually worked in knit stitches on a reverse stocking stitch background.

The contrast between the smooth knit stitches and the bumpy, dense purl side of the reverse stocking stitch allows the cable pattern to stand out clearly.

Cables can be simple, single braids or complex combinations of braids, honeycombs and plaits.

## Hints & tips

Cable needles come in straight versions, straight with a kink in the middle or occasionally hooked which can prevent stitches sliding off. Choose whichever works best for you If you don't have a cable needle handy, use a short DPN.

## Step 1

For a simple six-stitch cable that crosses to the left, purl to where the cable begins. Take a cable needle in the same (or slightly smaller) size as the main needles. Hold it in the RH, slightly above and parallel to the RH needle. Slip the next three stitches onto the cable needle as if you were going to purl them (p-wise).

## Step 2

Slide the slipped stitches (these will be worked later) along to the centre of the cable needle and hold the cable needle with stitches on to the front of the work. The cable needle can be supported in the RH as you work the next stitches or left loose at the front of the work. Alternatively, you can carefully poke it into the fabric but care should be taken not to split the yarn or snag the fabric.

## Step 3

Knit the next three stitches from LH main needle as normal. Avoid a hole at the crossover point by drawing up the yarn quite firmly after the first stitch. These stitches may feel tight and quite difficult to work. Don't worry, this is normal!

## Step 4

Next, work the stitches on the cable needle. Leave LH main needle at back of work. With cable needle in LH in front of the LH main needle, slide the stitches to the RH end of the cable needle. Be careful to keep the stitches in the same order and make sure you don't twist the stitches when lifting the needle.

## Step 5

This completes the LH-twisted cable. This type of cable may also be referred to in some patterns as a left cross, LH or front-cross cable.

## Step 6

For a cable that twists to the right, purl up to the point where the cable is to be made. Slip the next three stitches onto a cable needle. This time, hold the cable needle to the back of the work. Again, if it is easier, poke the needle through the knitted fabric, but being careful to avoid 'pulls'.

## Step 7

Knit the next three stitches from the LH main needle.

## Step 8

Now bring the cable needle to the front of the work, taking the LH main needle to the back. Be careful not to twist the stitches. Knit the three stitches from the cable needle in their original order.

## Step 9

This completes the right-twist cable (also referred to as a right cross, RH or back-cross cable). Depending on the pattern a number of 'plain' rows (rows with just knit and purl and no cabled or crossed stitches) may now be worked before the next cable row.

## Step 10

In this swatch a left-twist cable is combined with a right-twist cable to create a wave effect. Two cables are also worked at either end of the swatch. Each cable is separated by purl stitches and a purl band is worked at each edge to make the cables stand out. There is lots of fun to be had playing with cable combinations.

# Toys

A cuddly toy can be a friend for life, and hand-knitted ones are already full of love in every stitch. These cuties are sure to be a big hit with your little ones.

# Barnyard Pals

**1**

**Beginner**

The ideal size for little hands, this trio of friendly toys will give the lucky recipient as much pleasure at playtime as you'll get from knitting them.

This cow, sheep and donkey are just bursting with character – and we know you'll love bringing them to life. With one ball of each colour, you can make the sheep and the donkey or the cow – with two balls of each colour, you can make all three.

## Cow

**Legs** (make 4)

Leg starts from the top of the leg.

With MC1, cast on 20 sts.

Work in St st for 6 rows.

Change to MC2 and work in St st for 4 rows.

Purl 2 rows.

**Row 13:** *K1, k2tog, k1; rep from * to end. 15 sts.

**Row 14:** *P1, p2tog; rep from * to end. 10 sts.

**Row 15:** *K2tog; rep from * to end. 5 sts.

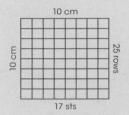

**CAST ON**

Break yarn and draw tail through rem sts, pull tight, and fasten.

**Body** (make 1)

Body starts from neck.

With MC1, cast on 10 sts.

**Row 1:** *Kfb; rep from * to end. 20 sts.

**Row 2:** Purl.

**Row 3:** *Kfb, k1; rep from * to end. 30 sts.

**Row 4:** Purl.

**Row 5:** *K1, kfb, k1; rep from * to end. 40 sts.

**Row 6:** Purl.

**Row 7:** *K1, kfb, k2; rep from * to end. 50 sts.

Work in St st for 15 rows.

**Row 23:** *K1, k2tog, k2; rep from * to end. 40 sts.

**Row 24:** Purl.

**Row 25:** *K1, k2tog, k1; rep from * to end. 30 sts.

**Row 26:** Purl.

**Row 27:** *K1, k2tog; rep from * to end. 20 sts.

**Row 28:** Purl.

## About this pattern

### Yarn

Lion Brand Superwash Merino Cashmere – 1–2 x 40g balls in Blossom (MC1) and 1–2 x 40g in Wine (MC2)

### About the Yarn

Aran; 80m per 40g ball; 72% Merino wool, 15% nylon, 13% cashmere

### Needles

5 mm, straight

### Tension

Measured over St st:

```
        10 cm
   ┌─────────────┐
10 │             │ 25
cm │             │ rows
   └─────────────┘
        17 sts
```

### Other supplies

Tapestry needle
Toy stuffing
Crochet hook to add hair

### Hints & tips

Pin the pieces of your animal together before sewing, just in case you find one ear is slightly out of place or if your animal topples over when you stand him up. To give your animal a flatter foot, cut out small cardboard circles and insert them in the leg before stuffing

**Row 29:** *K2tog; rep from * to end. 10 sts.

**Row 30:** *P2tog; rep from * to end. 5 sts.

Break yarn and draw tail through rem sts, pull tight, and fasten.

**Head** (make 1)

Head starts from top of head.

With MC1, cast on 12 sts.

**Row 1:** K1, [kfb] 4 times, k2, [kfb] 4 times, k1. 20 sts.

**Row 2:** Purl.

**Row 3:** K2, [kfb] 6 times, k4, [kfb] 6 times, k2. 32 sts.

Work in St st for 3 rows.

**Row 7:** K6, [kfb] 4 times, k12, [kfb] 4 times, k6. 40 sts.

Work in St st for 11 rows.

Change to MC2 and work in St st for 6 rows.

**Row 25:** K6, [k2tog] 4 times, k12, [k2tog] 4 times, k6. 32 sts.

**Row 26:** Purl.

**Row 27:** K2, [k2tog] 6 times, k4, [k2tog] 6 times, k2. 20 sts.

**Row 28:** Purl.

**Row 29:** K1, [k2tog] 4 times, k2, [k2tog] 4 times, k1. 12 sts.

Cast off.

**Ears** (make 2)

Ears start from bottom of ears.

With MC2, cast on 10 sts.

**Row 1:** K1, [kfb] twice, k4, [kfb] twice, k1. 14 sts.

Work in St st for 3 rows.

**Row 5:** K1, k2tog, k1, k2tog, k2, k2tog, k1, k2tog, k1. 10 sts.

**Row 6:** P1, [p2tog] 4 times, p1. 6 sts.

**Row 7:** K1, [k2tog] twice, k1. 4 sts.

**Row 8:** [P2tog] twice. 2 sts.

Cast off.

**Horns** (make 2)

With MC2, cast on 10 sts.

**Row 1:** K2tog, k2, [kfb] twice, k2, k2tog.

**Row 2:** Purl.

**Row 3:** [K2tog] twice, [kfb] twice, [k2tog] twice. 8 sts.

**Row 4:** Purl.

**Row 5:** K2tog, k1, [kfb] twice, k1, k2tog.

**Row 6:** Purl.

**Row 7:** *K2tog; rep from * to end. 4 sts.

**Row 8:** Purl.

**Row 9:** [K2tog] twice. 2 sts.

Cast off.

**Patch 1**

With MC2, cast on 6 sts.

**Row 1:** Cast on 1 st, k7. 7 sts.

**Row 2:** Cast on 1 st, p8. 8 sts.

**Row 3:** Cast on 3 sts, k11. 11 sts.

**Row 4:** Cast on 1 st, p12. 12 sts.

Work in St st for 2 rows.

**Row 7:** Cast off 4 sts, k7. 8 sts.

**Row 8:** Purl.

**Row 9:** Cast off 1 st, k6. 7 sts.

**Row 10:** Cast off 1 st, p5. 6 sts.

**Row 11:** Cast off 1 st, k4. 5 sts.

**Row 12:** Cast off 1 st, p3. 4 sts.

Cast off.

**Patch 2**

With MC2, cast on 6 sts.

**Row 1:** Purl.

**Row 2:** Cast on 2 sts, k8. 8 sts.

**Row 3:** Cast on 2 sts, p10. 10 sts.

Work in St st for 3 rows.

**Row 7:** Cast off 5 sts, k5. 5 sts.

**Row 8:** Purl.

Cast off.

**Tail** (make 1)

With MC1, cast on 10 sts.

Work in St st for 3 rows.

Cast off.

## Sheep

### Legs (make 4)

Leg starts at top of leg.

With MC2, cast on 16 sts.

Work in St st for 8 rows.

**Row 9:** Purl.

**Row 10:** *P1, p2tog, p1; rep from * to end. 12 sts.

**Row 11:** *K1, k2tog; rep from * to end. 8 sts.

**Row 12:** *P2tog; rep from * to end. 4 sts.

Break yarn and draw tail through rem sts, pull tight, and fasten.

### Body (make 1)

Body starts at top of neck.

With MC1, cast on 10 sts.

**Row 1:** *Kfb; rep from * to end. 20 sts.

**Row 2:** Purl.

**Row 3:** *Kfb, loop st; rep from * to end. 30 sts.

**Row 4:** Purl.

**Row 5:** *Loop st, kfb, k1; rep from * to end. 40 sts.

**Row 6:** Purl.

**Row 7:** *Loop st, k1; rep from * to end.

**Row 8:** Purl.

**CAST ON**

**Row 9:** *K1, loop st; rep from * to end.

Rep Rows 6–9 once, then rep Rows 6–8 once more.

**Row 17:** *K1, k2tog, loop st; rep from * to end. 30 sts.

**Row 18:** Purl.

**Row 19:** *K2tog, loop st; rep from * to end. 20 sts.

**Row 20:** Purl.

**Row 21:** *K2tog; rep from * to end. 10 sts.

**Row 22:** *P2tog; rep from * to end. 5 sts.

Break yarn and draw tail through rem sts, pull tight, and fasten.

### Head (make 1)

Head starts at top of head.

With MC2, cast on 8 sts.

**Row 1:** K1, [kfb] twice, k2, [kfb] twice, k1. 12sts.

**Row 2:** Purl.

**Row 3:** K1, [kfb] 3 times, k4, [kfb] 3 times, k1. 18 sts.

**Row 4:** Purl.

**Row 5:** K3, [kfb] 3 times, k6, [kfb] 3 times, k3. 24 sts.

**Row 6:** Purl.

**Row 7:** K4, [kfb] 4 times, k8, [kfb] 4 times, k4. 32 sts.

Work in St st for 9 rows.

**Row 17:** K4, [k2tog] 4 times, k8, [k2tog] 4 times, k4. 24 sts.

**Row 18:** Purl.

**Row 19:** K3, [k2tog] 3 times, k6, [k2tog] 3 times, k3. 18 sts.

**Row 20:** Purl.

**Row 21:** K1, [k2tog] 3 times, k4, [k2tog] 3 times, k1.12 sts.

**Row 22:** Purl.

**Row 23:** K1, [k2tog] twice, k2, [k2tog] twice, k1. 8 sts.

Break yarn and draw tail through rem sts, pull tight, and fasten.

### Ears (make 2)

Ears start at bottom of ears.

With MC2, cast on 10 sts.

**Row 1:** Purl.

**Row 2:** K1, [kfb] twice, k4, [kfb] twice, k1. 14 sts.

**Row 3:** Purl.

**Row 4:** K1, [k2tog] twice, k4, [k2tog] twice, k1. 10 sts.

**Row 5:** P1, [p2tog] 4 times, p1. 6 sts.

**Row 6:** K1, [k2tog] twice, k1. 4 sts.

**Row 7:** [P2tog] twice. 2 sts.

Cast off.

### Hair

With MC1, cast on 8 sts.

**Row 1:** Purl.

**Row 2:** [Loop st, k1] 4 times.

**Row 3:** Purl.

**Row 4:** [K1, loop st] 4 times.

Cast off.

## Donkey

**Legs** (make 4)

Work as for cow, casting on with MC2 then changing to MC1.

**Body** (make 1)

Body starts at neck.

With MC2, cast on 8 sts.

**Row 1:** *Kfb; rep from * to end. 16 sts.

**Row 2:** Purl.

**Row 3:** *K1, kfb; rep from * to end. 24 sts.

**Row 4:** Purl.

**Row 5:** *K1, kfb, k1; rep from * to end. 32 sts.

**Row 6:** Purl.

**Row 7:** *K1, kfb, k2; rep from * to end. 40 sts.

Work in St st for 15 rows.

**Row 23:** *K1, k2tog, k2; rep from * to end. 32 sts.

**Row 24:** Purl.

**Row 25:** *K1, k2tog, k1; rep from * to end. 24 sts.

**Row 26:** Purl.

**Row 27:** *K1, k2tog; rep from * to end. 16 sts.

**Row 28:** Purl.

**Row 29:** *K2tog; rep from * to end. 8 sts.

**Row 30:** *P2tog; rep from * to end. 4 sts.

Break yarn and draw tail through rem sts, pull tight, and fasten.

**CAST ON**

## Head (make 1)

Head starts at top of head.

With MC2, cast on 10 sts.

**Row 1:** Purl.

**Row 2:** *K1, kfb; rep from * to end. 15 sts.

Work in St st for 3 rows.

**Row 6:** *K1, kfb, k1; rep from * to end. 20 sts.

**Row 7:** Purl.

**Row 8:** *K1, kfb, k2; rep from * to end. 25 sts.

**Row 9:** Purl.

**Row 10:** *K2, kfb, k2; rep from * to end. 30 sts.

**Row 11:** Purl.

Change to MC1.

**Row 12:** *K5, kfb ; rep from * to end. 35 sts.

**Row 13 and all odd rows:** Purl.

**Row 14:** *K3, kfb, k3; rep from * to end. 40 sts.

**Row 16:** *K2, kfb, k1; rep from * to end. 50 sts.

**Row 18:** *K4, k2tog, k4; rep from * to end. 45 sts.

**Row 20:** *K2, k2tog, k1; rep from * to end. 36 sts.

**Row 22:** *K1, k2tog, k1; rep from * to end. 27 sts.

**Row 24:** *K1, k2tog, k1; rep from * to end. 18 sts.

**Row 26:** *K2tog; rep from * to end. 9 sts.

Break yarn and draw tail through rem sts, pull tight, and fasten.

**Tail**

Work as for cow.

**Ears** (make 2)

Work as for cow.

## Schematics

### Cow

Floor to top of horns: 13 cm

Nose to tail: Approx. 20 cm

### Sheep

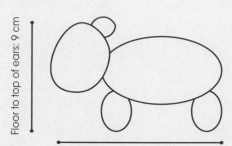

Floor to top of ears: 9 cm

Nose to bottom: Approx. 11 cm

### Donkey

Floor to top of ears: 9 cm

Nose to tail: Approx. 18 cm

40

### Making up

For all animals sew up the seam of the head, leaving a gap for stuffing and attaching eyes. For a neat result use mattress stitch.

To make the eyes, make a French knot and attach it in place. Check that both eyes are level.

Stuff and sew along the seam of the body. Stuff the legs and attach them to the body using pins.

Attach the head with pins and check the animal stands without support. Now sew the pieces together.

Secure the tail to the cow and the donkey and add some strands of hair by cutting lengths of yarn that are twice as long as you want the finished hair to be plus a little more, to allow for the knot and a final trim.

Insert a crochet hook into the back of the tail and put a folded strand of yarn on the hook.

Pull the loop through and then take the two ends of yarn and pull them through the loop to create a knot.

Repeat a few more times and trim the tail.

Repeat the same technique to the top of the donkey's head to give him his mane and trim to your desire.

For the sheep, sew the loopy hair piece to the top of his head.

To create the horns and ears, fold these in half and sew along the seam. Attach to the head using the cast on seam. Add the patches to the cow.

Your barnyard pals are now ready to wreak havoc in your home!

## Special instructions

**Loop stitch:**
To make a loop, knit one stitch like normal but instead of dropping the yarn off the left needle like a normal knit stitch, leave on LH needle. Bring the yarn from back to front in between needles and loop it around your thumb. Bring the yarn tail back between the needles and knit the stitch off the LH needle. You now have 2 sts on RH needle and a loop in between. Now pass the first st over the second st to secure the loop.

# Fuzzy Bear

A beloved teddy is a friend for life – but he needn't take that long to knit! Using simple shaping techniques, you can make this little guy in a few days.

The yarn is what makes this project absolutely perfect – the mohair content in Rowan Kid Classic gives Fuzzy Bear his name. He's quite easy to make, but if you want to make an even easier bear, skip the change of colour on his belly. The teddy is knit from the bottom up, and the body and head are knit in one piece.

## Body and head

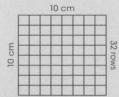
**CAST ON**

With MC, cast on 10 sts.

**Row 1 (and all WS rows unless otherwise noted):** Purl.

**Row 2 (RS):** K1, [kfb] nine times. 19 sts.

**Row 4:** K1, [kfb, k2] six times. 25 sts.

**Row 6:** K1, [kfb, k3] six times. 31 sts.

**Row 8:** K1, [kfb, k4] six times. 37 sts.

**Row 10:** K1, [kfb, k5] six times. 43 sts.

**Row 12:** K1, [kfb, k6] six times. 49 sts.

**Row 13:** P18, join CC and p12, join another ball of MC and purl to end.

**Row 14:** With MC k1, [kfb, k7] twice, kfb; with CC k7, kfb, k6; with MC k1, [kfb, k7] twice. 55 sts.

**Row 15:** With MC p18; with CC p17; with MC p20.

**Row 16:** With MC k20; with CC k17; with MC k18.

Rep Rows 15 and 16 five times more, then Row 15 once more.

**Row 28:** With MC [k8, k2tog] twice, k1; with CC k7, k2tog, k6; with MC k2, k2tog, k15. 51 sts.

**Row 29:** With MC p14, p2tog, p3; with CC p4, p2tog, p6; with MC p1, p2tog, p7, p2tog, p8. 47 sts.

**Row 30:** With MC k8, k2tog, k6, k2tog, k1; with CC k5, k2tog, k2; with MC k4, k2tog, k13. 43 sts.

**Row 31:** With MC p19; with CC p6; with MC p18.

Break CC (and extra MC) and continue in MC only.

**Row 32:** K1, [k2tog, k5] six times. 37 sts.

**Row 34:** K1, [k2tog, k4] six times. 31 sts.

**Row 36:** K1, [k2tog, k3] six times. 25 sts.

**Row 38:** K1, [kfb, k3] six times. 31 sts.

**Row 39:** [P4, pfb] six times, p1. 37 sts.

**Row 40:** K1, [kfb, k5] six times. 43 sts.

**Row 42:** K1, [kfb, k6] six times. 49 sts.

**Row 44:** K1, [kfb, k7] six times. 55 sts.

**Row 46:** K1, [kfb, k8] six times. 61 sts.

**Rows 48, 50, 52, 54:** Knit.

**Row 56:** K1, [k2tog, k8] six times. 55 sts.

**Row 58:** K1, [k2tog, k7] six times. 49 sts.

## About this pattern

### Yarn
Rowan Kid Classic – 1 x 50g ball in Bear 817 (MC) and 1 x 50g ball in Straw 851 (CC)

### About the yarn
DK weight; 140m per 50g ball; 70% lambswool, 26% mohair, 4% nylon

### Needles
3.75mm straight

### Tension
Measured over St st:

10 cm

10 cm

32 rows

24 sts

### Other supplies
Tapestry needle
Polyester fibrefill
9mm safety eyes
15mm safety nose

### Special instructions
**Pfb:** Purl through the front and then through the back of the same stitch.

**Row 60:** K1, [k2tog, k6] six times. 43 sts.

**Row 62:** K1, [k2tog, k5] six times. 37 sts.

**Row 64:** K1, [k2tog, k4] six times. 31 sts.

**Row 66:** K1, [k2tog, k3] six times. 25 sts.

**Row 67:** [P2, p2tog] six times, p1. 19 sts.

**Row 68:** K1, [k2tog, k1] six times. 13 sts.

Break yarn and draw tail through rem sts, pull tight, and fasten.

Using mattress stitch, seam the body, leaving a hole at the bottom open.

## Ears (make 2)

With MC, cast on 22 sts.

**Rows 1, 3, 5 (RS):** With MC k11; with CC k11.

**Rows 2, 4, 6:** With CC p11; with MC p11.

**Row 7:** With MC k1, [k2tog] five times; with CC [k2tog] five times, k1. 12 sts.

**Row 8:** With CC [p2tog] three times; with MC [p2tog] three times. 6 sts.

Cut CC and fasten on the WS. Break MC, leaving long tail. Draw tail through rem sts, pull tight, and fasten.

Fold the ear with the wrong sides facing. Seam down the side.

## Muzzle

With CC, cast on 25 sts.

**Row 1 (RS):** Knit.

**Row 2 and all WS rows:** Purl.

**Row 3:** As Row 1.

**Row 5:** K1, [k2tog, k1] eight times. 17 sts.

**Row 7:** K1, [k2tog] eight times. 9 sts.

**Row 9:** K1, [k2tog] four times. 5 sts.

Break yarn, leaving long tail. Draw tail through rem sts, pull tight, and fasten. Seam down the side. Attach safety nose or embroider nose to middle of muzzle.

## Arms (make 2)

With MC, cast on 10 sts.

**Row 1 and all WS rows (WS):** Purl.

**Row 2:** K1, [kfb k2] three times. 13 sts.

**Row 4:** K1, [kfb, k3] three times. 16 sts.

**Row 6:** K1, [kfb, k4] three times. 19 sts.

**Rows 8, 10, 12, 14, 16:** Knit.

**Row 18:** K1, [k2tog, k1] six times. 13 sts.

**Row 20:** K1, [k2tog] six times. 7 sts.

Break yarn, leaving long tail. Draw tail through rem sts, pull tight, and fasten. Fold the arm with the wrong sides facing. Using mattress stitch, seam down the side. Stuff and seam across the top.

## Legs (make 2)

With MC, cast on 16 sts.

Beginning with a knit row, work in St st for 20 rows.

**Row 21:** K5, [kfb] seven times, k4. 23 sts.

**Row 22:** Purl.

Work in St st for 4 rows.

**Row 27:** K5, [k2tog] seven times, k4. 16 sts.

**Row 28:** [P2tog] eight times. 8 sts.

Break yarn, leaving long tail. Draw tail through rem sts, pull tight, and fasten. Fold the leg with the wrong sides facing. Using mattress stitch, seam down the side. Stuff. If you want your bear to be able to sit, seam across the top of the leg, with the foot facing you.

**Finishing:** Stuff body. Using mattress stitch, attach the muzzle to the centre of the face. Stuff the muzzle before it is fully attached. Add the safety eyes, or embroider eyes, about 4 sts up from the muzzle and 3 sts apart. Attach ears to the side of the head, with the bottom of the ears level with the eyes. Seam up the hole at the bottom of body and attach arms and legs to sides and base of body.

## Schematic

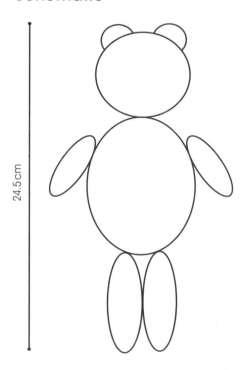

24.5cm

## Hints & tips

When working the intarsia part for the tummy, remember to twist the yarn together at the colour changes so you do not get a hole. Before you start knitting, wind some of the main colour into a separate ball so you have a ball for either side of the colour change.

# Drawstring Bag & Pouch

These little knitted pouches are great for adding a splash of colour to your baby kit or for storing toys.

Simple stripes are fun to knit and we love the way these colours play together in stripes. If you have scraps of DK yarn in your stash, this would be an ideal pattern for using them all up.

## Drawstring bag

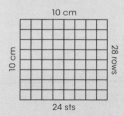

**CAST ON**

Using blue yarn, cast on 77 sts.

Work in St st in stripes as follows:

6 rows blue, then **6 rows green, 2 rows cream, 2 rows red, 6 rows blue, 2 rows green, 6 rows cream, 6 rows red** then 2 rows blue. Rep from ** to ** once more.

Break off all yarn except blue and cont in blue only.

Knit 1 row.

**Dec row:** K2, k2tog, *k6, k2tog; rep from * to last st, k1. 67 sts.

Knit 10 rows.

**Eyelet row:** K4, k2tog, yo, *k6, k2tog, yo; rep from * to last 5 sts, k5.

Knit 12 rows.

Cast off k-wise.

## i-cord

Using green, cast on 2 sts.

Work i-cord for 55cm.

Cast off.

Sew in ends. Join side seams. Placing seam at centre back, join bottom seam.

Thread i-cord through eyelets and tie in a bow.

## About this pattern

**2**

**Intermediate**

### Yarn

1 ball each in Blueberry Muffin, Peppermint Green, Vanilla Slice and Strawberry Fool

This is enough to knit both the bag and the pouch

### About the Yarn

Betty and Belle DK; DK; 75m per 25g ball; 100% acrylic

### Needles

4mm straight

### Tension

Measured over St st:

10 cm

10 cm

28 rows

24 sts

### Other supplies

Tapestry needle

Yarn bobbin (optional)

### i-cord

K all sts on DPN. Without turning, slide sts to other end of needle. Rep until cord reaches desired length.

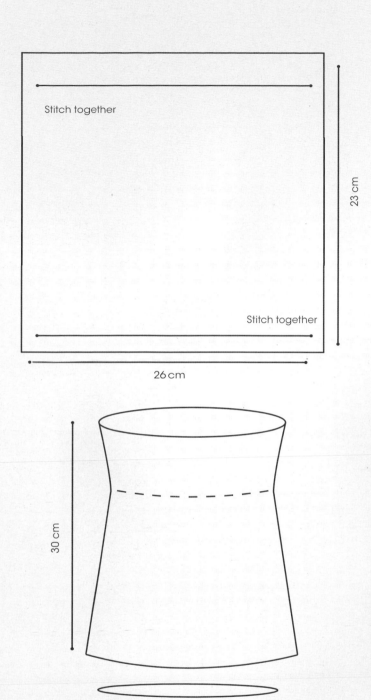

Stitch together

23 cm

Stitch together

26 cm

30 cm

30 cm

## Pouch

Before you start, wind off a small amount of green into a second ball or bobbin.

Using the main ball of green, cast on 63 sts.

**\*\*Row 1 (RS):** Using green, knit.

**Row 2:** Using green, k6, p to last 6 sts, k6.

**Row 3:** K6 green, k51 blue, k6 green using smaller ball/bobbin.

**Row 4:** K6 green, p51 blue, k6 green.

Keeping 6 sts at each end in green and G st, work centre 51 sts in St st stripes of 6 rows in red, 2 rows in cream, 6 rows in green, 2 rows in blue, 6 rows in red, 2 rows in cream\*\* then 8 rows in green, and finally rep from \*\* to \*\* but reversing the order of stripes.

Cast off.

## i-cords (make 2)

Using red, cast on 2 sts.

Work i-cord for 20cm.

Cast off.

Sew in ends.

With WS facing, join side seams for approximately 5cm at each end. Placing open seam at centre front, join side seams. Turn pouch inside out.

Sew i-cords across G st at each side of gap and tie in a bow.

## Special instructions

i-cord can be knitted on two needles as follows:

Cast on 2 sts.

**Row 1:** K2,\*sl these 2 sts back onto left-hand needle, k2, rep from \* until work measures required length.

Cast off.

Changing colours: twist yarns together at back of work to prevent a hole forming.